73
f
mf
79
f
85
p
91

CONTENTS

Volume I

1	J. Haydn	Minuet, from Twelve Minuets for keyboard published in 1785
2	F. Couperin	Les Graces-Naturelles, from Keyboard Suite No. 11
3	F. Schubert	Andantino, from the incidental music to *Rosamunde*
4	P. Tchaikovsky	Reverie, from *The Album for the Young,* Opus 39
5	L. van Beethoven	Bagatelle, No 9 from the Bagatelles for piano, Opus 119
6	H. Purcell	Minuet, from Keyboard Suite No. 5 in C
7	G. F. Handel	Air, from Keyboard Suite No. 5 in E
8	J. Haydn	Allegretto, from String Quartet Opus 74, No. 2
9	F. Couperin	Menuet, from Keyboard Suite No. 3
10	R. Schumann	Sheherazade, from *The Album for the Young*, Opus 68

Volume II

1	F. Couperin	Passepied, from Keyboard Suite No. 2
2	J. Haydn	Allegro, from Piano Sonata No. 5 in C
3	J. Brahms	Waltz, from the waltzes for piano, Opus 39
4	J. Brahms	Waltz, from the waltzes for piano, Opus 39
5	F. Schubert	Ballet, from the incidental music to *Rosamunde*
6	R. Schumann	Reconnaissance, from *Carnival,* Opus 9
7	E. Grieg	Waltz, from *Lyric Pieces*, Opus 71
8	P. Tchaikovsky	The Lark's Song, from *The Album for the Young,* Opus 39

Extra flute parts are on sale separately.

3. Waltz

(Opus 39,No.1)

J. Brahms

20
mf
27
mp
mf
35
mf
p
43
p

2. Allegro

J. Haydn

THE BEGINNER'S REPERTOIRE FOR FLUTE

Vol. II

Selected and adapted by
IVAN C. PHILLIPS

1. Passepied

Printed in Great Britain
OXFORD UNIVERSITY PRESS, MUSIC DEPARTMENT, WALTON STREET, OXFORD OX2 6DP

26
p
mf
32
ff
37
f
43
p

4. Waltz
(Opus 39,No. 2)

J. Brahms

50
f
1.
2.
55
60
fz
cresc.
p
66

5. Ballet

(from *Rosamunde*)

F. Schubert

28
R.H.
35
41
fp
48
pp
pp

6. Reconnaissance

(from *Carnival*)

R. Schumann

THE BEGINNER'S REPERTOIRE FOR FLUTE
Vol. II

Selected and adapted by
IVAN C. PHILLIPS

Flute

1. Passepied

Allegretto

F. Couperin

Printed in Great Britain

OXFORD UNIVERSITY PRESS, MUSIC DEPARTMENT, WALTON STREET, OXFORD OX2 6DP

Flute

2. Allegro

J. Haydn

Flute

3. Waltz

(Opus 39,No.1)

J. Brahms

Flute

4. Waltz

(Opus 39,No.2)

J. Brahms

5. Ballet

(from *Rosamunde*)

F. Schubert

Andante un poco mosso

Flute

6. Reconnaissance

(from *Carnival*)

R. Schumann

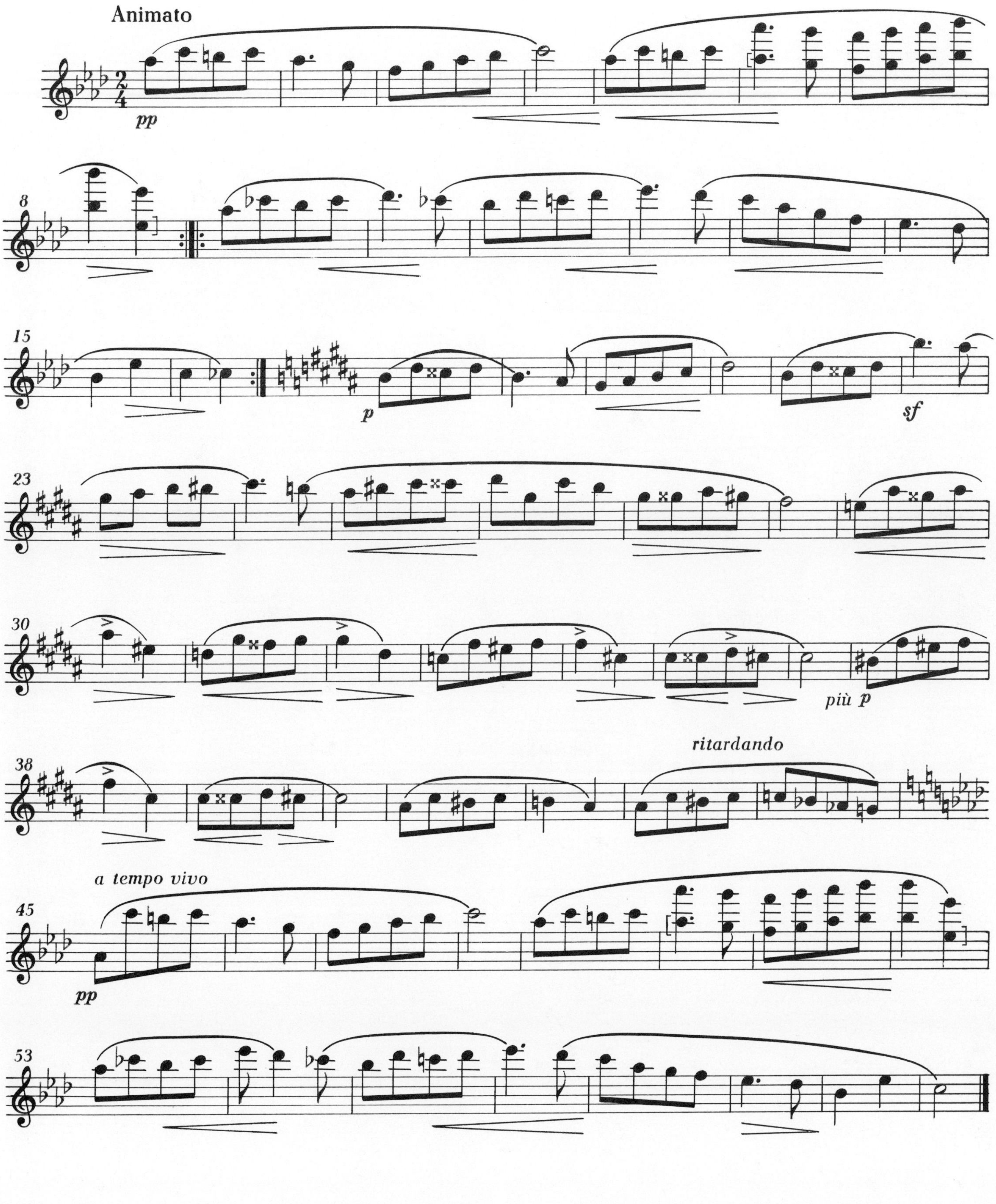

Flute

7. Waltz

(Opus 71.No,7)

Tempo di Valse

E. Grieg

Flute

8. The Lark's Song

(Opus 39,No.22)

P. Tchaikovsky

21
sf
26
30
dim.
35
più p
più p

40
ritardando
dim – in – u – en – do
45
a tempo vivo
pp
pp a tempo vivo staccato
50
55

7. Waltz
(Opus 71,No.7)

Tempo di Valse

E. Grieg

23
a tempo
poco rti.
3
pp dolce
poco rit.
pp dolce a tempo
29
pp
pp
36
43
cresc.
cresc. molto
f
poco rit.
cresc.
cresc. molto
f

49
a tempo
p
p a tempo
56
63
69
rit. al fine
pp
rit. al fine
Ped

8. The Lark's Song

(Opus 39,No.22)

P. Tchaikovsky

Reproduced and printed by
Halstan & Co. Ltd., Amersham, Bucks., England